DAVID ROBINSON

NBA SUPER CENTER

BY BILL GUTMAN

MILLBROOK SPORTS WORLD

THE MILLBROOK PRESS

BROOKFIELD, CONNECTICUT

Published by The Millbrook Press
2 Old New Milford Road
Brookfield, CT 06804

Created in association with Grey Castle Press, Inc.
Series Editorial Director: *Elizabeth Simon*
Art Director: *Nancy Driscoll*
Design Management: *Italiano-Perla Design*

Photographs courtesy of: John W. McDonough: cover, 3, 43, 44, 46;
Phil Hoffmann: 4, 13, 18; U.S. Navy: 7; Princess Anne Junior High
School: 10; Osbourn Park High School: 12; AP/Wide World Photos: 17,
20, 23, 25, 26, 29, 31, 38, 40; *San Antonio Light:* 36-37.

Library of Congress Cataloging-in-Publication Data

Gutman, Bill.
David Robinson, NBA super center / by Bill Gutman.
p. cm. — (Millbrook sports world)
Includes bibliographical references (p. 46) and index.
Summary: A biography of the Naval Academy's star basketball
player and member of the 1988 Olympic team, who has gone on to
play with the San Antonio Spurs.
ISBN 1-56294-228-X
1. Robinson, David, 1965 —Juvenile literature.
2. Basketball players—United States—
Biography—Juvenile literature.
[1. Robinson, David 1965- . 2. Basketball players. 3. Afro-
Americans—Biography] I. Title. II. Series.
GV884.R615G88 1993
796.323'092—dc20
[B]
92-18164 CIP AC

DAVID ROBINSON

Most people felt that time was running out for the United States Naval Academy basketball team. It was the second round of the 1986 National Collegiate Athletic Association (NCAA) Tournament, and Navy's Midshipmen were up against Syracuse University. Navy had played Syracuse during the regular season and had lost by a whopping 22 points. No one had any reason to think that the Middies would play better this time. With a pair of All-American players in center Rony Seikaly and guard Dwayne "Pearl" Washington, the Syracuse Orangemen were heavy favorites to win the game and send Navy out of the tournament.

But Navy had a star player as well. His name was David Robinson, and before the game was over both the Syracuse team and the rest of the basketball world would find out just how very good the Midshipman star had become.

David first gained national attention during the 1986 NCAA tournament in his junior year at the Naval Academy.

David Robinson was a 6-foot-11 (211-centimeter) center in his third year at the Naval Academy. He was a big man who could run, score, rebound, and block shots. Against Syracuse he put on a show that is still remembered by those who saw it. Robinson played very well during the entire first half. Because of his scoring and rebounding, Navy had a slim lead early in the second half. But Syracuse was starting to run and fast break. It looked as if they might be ready to take control of the game.

David Robinson didn't let it happen. He got the ball down low and hit yet another hoop for the Middies. Instead of high-fiving teammates and taking a quick breather, his eyes scanned the court to pick up the action. As he expected, Syracuse was trying to fast break. Pearl Washington had the ball and was racing down court. The middle was open, and it looked as if Pearl would go in for an easy layup.

Suddenly, there was Robinson. He had run down the speedy Washington from behind. He soared through the air over Washington and blocked the shot cleanly from behind. His momentum carried him over the end line and out of bounds. Wendell Alexis of Syracuse grabbed the loose ball and tried to put up another shot from underneath. Once again Robinson seemed to come out of nowhere. He came leaping back in from out of bounds and blocked Alexis's shot beautifully. This time Navy got the ball, went on a fast break of its own, and scored.

"Whenever I think back about David and our team during those years, I always think of that sequence," said Navy guard Doug Wojcik, one of David's teammates. "It really showed what David was all about. The whole series of plays with the two blocks was so impressive."

The two Robinson blocks set the tone for the rest of the game. Navy finished with a big 97-85 win, as Robinson scored 35 points and grabbed 11 rebounds. The team would eventually lose in the Regional Final, but they had gone farther than any Navy team before them. That's because Navy had never had a player as good as David Robinson. As Syracuse coach Jim Boeheim put it:

"[David] is as good a big man as there is in the country. He just killed us."

NAVY UPBRINGING

David Maurice Robinson had been around the Navy all his life. His father, Ambrose Robinson, was a career Navy man. He was a sonar technician and a petty officer who was sometimes away at sea for six months at a time.

David was born on August 6, 1965. He was the second of the three Robinson children. David, his sister Kim, and brother Chuck all grew up in Virginia Beach, Virginia. That's because Virginia Beach was very close to the huge naval base at Norfolk, Virginia, where Mr. Robinson was stationed.

David grew up in Virginia Beach, Virginia, near the huge Naval Base at Norfolk, shown in this aerial photo.

David's mother, Freda Robinson, worked as a nurse, so there were times when both his parents were away at the same time. All three Robinson children learned to fend for themselves. Their parents would leave very precise instructions for them. The children always had chores to do and responsibilities around the house. Some of them included cooking, cleaning, housework, and gardening. And they always had their homework to do.

"We had a lot of responsibilities as children, but we had freedom, too," David said. "For that reason, I never felt any desire to break loose. And we always knew the difference between right and wrong."

Unlike a lot of kids, David enjoyed discipline and routine. Maybe his father's naval training was rubbing off on him. He also showed he was very bright at an early age. At the supermarket he would figure the amount of the groceries before his mother reached the cash register.

When he entered the first grade, David was put in a special program for gifted children. He would remain an outstanding student right up to his graduation from the Naval Academy. He always liked school and never complained about doing homework or studying.

Whenever David's father was home, the whole family did things together. They might go fishing or bowling. Sometimes they went on vacations. They also played a lot of different sports, but just for fun.

As he grew older, he began spending more and more time with his father. Ambrose Robinson was a tall man, standing 6 feet 6 (198 centimeters). He had many interests and loved to work around his house. He could build or repair almost anything. Young David watched him and learned.

"My Dad was the person I patterned myself after," David said. "I never had any sports role models as a youngster. To me, my Dad was everything."

Soon it was like father, like son. David was curious about everything. He took things apart to see how they worked and tried to repair them when they were broken. When he was 12, he set up and installed a wide-screen television as a surprise for his mother. His father had brought it home, but then received orders to ship out. Instead of waiting for his father to get back, David took over and did the job. He already had the self-confidence to do whatever he put his mind to.

David was special in other ways too. By the time he was 14 he was taking advanced computer courses at school. He was also teaching himself to play the piano and French horn by ear. His favorite subject in school was math.

For David it was a happy childhood. "I never realized what a good life I was leading until I began making friends with guys who didn't even talk to their parents or brothers and sisters," he said. "I know now how much they are missing, all that love."

The one thing that wasn't a big part of David's early life was sports. Playing sports of any kind was something he did for fun once in a while. At Princess Anne Junior High he played basketball for part of one year, but he wasn't one of these kids who played ball from morning until night. He had no real passion for sports. And that wouldn't change for quite some time.

HIGH SCHOOL YEARS

David continued to be a top student. In the fall of 1979 he entered Green Run High School in Virginia Beach. He was a shade over 6 feet (183 centimeters) then and decided to go out for the basketball team. But he didn't stay long. Within a short time he quit. He felt he wasn't good enough.

David went out for basketball as a freshman at Green Run High in 1979.
In this team photo David is in the back row, seventh from the left, directly
under the basket. The coach kneeling on the left is Herman Reid, the father
of former North Carolina star and current NBA player J.R. Reid.

Green Run was a large high school with too many good players. David was just starting to grow then. By his sophomore year he was already 6 feet 4 (193 centimeters), but there were other kids just as tall who were better. Had he stayed at Green Run all four years he might never have played. But in the fall of 1982, shortly after he started his senior year, the Robinsons moved.

Ambrose Robinson had retired from the Navy after 20 years of service. He got a job in the northern part of Virginia and in November moved his family to Manassas. Manassas was in the Washington, D.C. area, and David would be going to Osbourn Park High School. By then he was nearly 6 feet 7 (201 centimeters). When a kid that tall comes into a school, the basketball coach hears about it quickly.

The coach was Art Payne, and he asked David if he wanted to come out for the team. David said maybe. Then a lot of the other kids began to urge him to play. So he finally agreed. Once he decided to join the team he practiced very hard.

"He never missed a practice, never missed a game," said Coach Payne. "And he was a super young man to work with."

But he wasn't yet a great player. By the time players like Magic Johnson and Michael Jordan were seniors in high school, they were so good that every college in the country wanted them. David's goal was to attend the Naval Academy. He didn't give a career in basketball a second thought.

"I never played much street ball," David said, "so I didn't have the moves, the natural instincts for the game that kids learn over the years on the playgrounds."

David became the starting center when the team's regular center got hurt. Coach Payne said he knew David could be a quality player, but he had an awful lot to learn. Osbourn Park was in a tough league and finished the year with a 12-12 record. Even though David averaged about 14 points a game to lead the team, his playing still wasn't consistent.

Coach Payne said he didn't have a real shooting touch and rebounded well only because of his size. But he had soft hands and caught the ball well. He was also very graceful when running up and down the court. Would he become a star? No one really knew.

This yearbook photo shows David as a senior at Osbourn Park High in Manassas, Virginia. He is in the center of the back row.

David continued to be a star in the classroom. That was what was most important to him. When David received his score on the college board exams he was overjoyed. He had scored 1,320 out of a possible 1,600 points. Shortly afterward, he received his appointment to the United States Naval Academy.

David felt the Academy had one of the best math programs in the country. That would be his major. He also said that he knew he would be successful in life if he graduated from the Naval Academy. But the basketball coaches at the Academy were only interested in his performance on the court. He was 6 feet 7 (201 centimeters) when he applied to Navy, but the height limit for the Academy was 6 feet 6 (198 centimeters). Luckily, another rule stated that five percent of the incoming class could be as tall as 6 feet 8 (203 centimeters).

So David had made it to the Academy by just one inch. Yet no one had any idea what would happen with this new recruit in the next four years.

THE MAKING OF A STAR

While David went to the Naval Academy in the late summer of 1983 as a first-year student, the basketball coaches had other ideas. Pete Herrmann, who was an assistant when David entered and would later become head coach, saw the freshman as a player with potential.

"We thought David could become a solid running forward," said Herrmann. "His hands were pretty good and he could run. He needed more strength and stamina, but that was something he could develop. What none of us knew back then was that he could become a center."

While the rest of the country knew David as a basketball All-American, at the Naval Academy he spent as much time working at his computer as he did on the basketball court.

By the time David came out for basketball he had grown some more. He was now 6 feet 9 (206 centimeters) and getting taller. But he still didn't have a real love of the sport and his coaches saw that. Pete Herrmann said he couldn't even remember David doing anything special in practice that year. He was just another player.

David struggled on the court all year. There was so much to learn about the game. He studied the other players and kept practicing. Slowly he got better. Navy had a hustling team that went 24-8 in David's freshman year. He played about 13 minutes a game and averaged 7.6 points. But he had an outstanding 62.3 shooting percentage and blocked 37 shots.

During the summer David lifted weights and played in a summer league in Washington, D.C. When he returned for his sophomore year he surprised everyone. He had grown another two inches and was now 6 feet 11 (211 centimeters). He had also put on 20 pounds (9 kilograms) and now weighed 215 (98 kilograms). There was no doubt he was a full-fledged center.

Navy had some other good players coming back. Forwards Vernon Butler and Kylor Whitaker and guard Doug Wojcik were very solid. If David could handle the job at center, Navy might have a very good team.

Of course, David's schoolwork still came first. He was a math major and had courses such as thermodynamics, physics, navigation, computer science, and advanced calculus. None of those would be easy, and David knew he would really have to balance his time. But David always did very well with his studies.

When it was time for basketball again he felt he was ready. The Middies' coach, Paul Evans, decided early that David was the most important player on the team. Evans wanted to have the offense revolve around the big center. That put a lot of pressure on David, but he didn't seem to mind. Pete Herrmann remembers how the offense worked.

"We simply moved the ball into David," Coach Herrmann said. "We left him in the same spot and got the ball to him. It was a tribute to both Coach Evans and to David that it worked. We told David not to try too many things inside. Just catch the ball and score. For most of his sophomore year he kept it on the simple side."

In the third game of the 1984-1985 season, David began to fulfill his potential. He exploded for 29 points as Navy topped American University, 84-68. He was becoming more than just another tall kid. He was starting to become a basketball player. A short time later, Navy traveled to Southern Illinois as part of a four-team Saluki Shootout tournament. In the first game David had a career-best 31 points, but the Middies lost to host Southern Illinois, 75-72. Then came the consolation game against Western Illinois.

Suddenly David Robinson was on fire. He was the dominant player at both ends of the floor. He was scoring on a variety of turnaround jump shots, drives, and dunks. At the other end he was soaring above everyone to corral rebound after rebound. When it ended, Navy had an 80-74 victory, and David had 37 points along with 18 rebounds. For his effort he was named the Most Valuable Player of the entire tournament.

The word was getting out—David Robinson was becoming a special player. And Navy continued to win. In fact, the team won ten straight games after the tournament. Against East Carolina David had another career high of 39 points. He had become the key to the team's success.

"Not many 6-foot-11 centers have his hands, his shooting touch, and his ability to run the floor," Coach Evans said. "David can block a shot at one end and dunk at the other."

With David leading the way, Navy had its best season in history. The Middies finished the season at 26-6 and received their first bid to the NCAA Tournament in 25 years. That's when Navy showed they could play any team. The Middies upset Louisiana State before losing a close game to Maryland. The Maryland team double- and triple-teamed David the entire game. As one writer said, "It was the first time Goliath ever got frightened by David."

But it was David who was becoming the Goliath. His scoring average went from 7.6 points a game as a freshman to leading the team with 23.6 points a game his sophomore year. He was also the Middies' best rebounder with an 11.6 average. In addition, he blocked 128 shots and was named the Eastern Collegiate Athletic Conference (ECAC) South Player of the Year.

There was little doubt that he was now a top-flight center and on the verge of becoming a star.

ALL-AMERICAN

No one had expected David Robinson to become a basketball force. In fact no one expected him to be a 7-footer (213-centimeter), but he was almost that tall when he returned to the Academy in the fall of 1985. While more and more people thought his future was in basketball, Academy Superintendent Rear Admiral Charles R. Larson talked about the total person David had become.

"David Robinson is the kind of kid the Naval Academy would go after if he couldn't play basketball at all. He's an excellent student and a natural leader. That's what we look for here."

David had played summer league ball in Spain and was more than ready when his junior season began. He now weighed a solid 230 pounds (104 kilograms) and was still growing. The Middies opened the 1985-1986 season against a powerful St. John's team at Madison Square Garden in New York. Although the Redmen won 66-58, David was brilliant. He scored 27 points and grabbed 18 rebounds. Many people were beginning to think Navy had the best player.

After the opening loss, Navy won 14 of their next 16 games. David continued his outstanding play. He was leading the nation in blocked shots and was among the leaders in rebounding. In a January game against North Carolina-Wilmington, David blocked an amazing total of 14 shots. Many opposing players began stay-

As a junior at the Naval Academy, David was beginning to dominate games. Here he grabs one of 25 rebounds, a school record, in a win over Fairfield University.

ing out of the middle. They knew if they drove to the hoop, David would be there for the block.

This was a very good Navy team. The Middies won their conference tournament and moved on to the NCAA championship tournament. In the first round they whipped Tulsa 87-68, as David scored 30 points and grabbed 12 rebounds. Next came the tough Syracuse team. Led by guard Pearl Washington and center Rony Seikaly, Syracuse was the heavy favorite.

But this time it was different. David dominated the game at both ends. This was the game in which he had an outstanding offensive and defensive sequence. He scored a hoop, stopped a Syracuse fast break with two great blocks, then started a Navy break that led to another hoop. After that, it was Navy all the way. Navy won the game 97-85, with David scoring 35 points and taking down 11 rebounds.

After beating Cleveland State 71-70, the team had gone farther in the NCAA tournament than any Navy ball club ever had. Next came the East regional final against Duke at the Meadowlands Arena in New Jersey. The winner would be going to the fabled Final Four. Although many thought Navy would win, Duke just had too much quickness for the Midshipmen. Led by guard Johnny Dawkins, who scored 28, the Blue Devils won it, 71-50. David ended his junior season scoring 23 points and grabbing 10 rebounds.

By the time David was a senior he had grown to be 7 feet (213 centimeters) tall. It wasn't easy for him to get through the doors of one of the training ships at the Academy.

The 1985-1986 season had still been a great one for Navy. The team finished with a 30-5 record, the best in its history. David averaged 22.7 points a game and led the nation in both rebounding and blocked shots. He had 455 rebounds for a 13.0 average and a record 207 blocked shots. That was an amazing number. Of all the teams in the country, only national champ Louisville blocked more shots as a team than David had by himself. The Louisville team blocked 213 shots.

After the season, David was named a first team All-American in several polls and was a second-team selection on many more. He had become an outstanding player and an All-American. And he still had one more year to go.

PLAYER OF THE YEAR

During the summer of 1986, David led the United States National Team to a victory in the World Championships in Spain. He was now a full 7 feet tall (213 centimeters) and still growing. In the world championships he outplayed Russia's best big man, Arvidas Sabonis, a player thought good enough to be in the NBA.

By the time David reported for his first basketball practice at Navy in the fall, he was 7 feet 1 (216 centimeters) and weighed 235 pounds (107 kilograms). He had grown six inches since entering the Academy. Pete

In the summer of 1986, David played for the United States national team at the World Basketball Championships in Madrid, Spain. In a game against the Soviet Union, David outplayed Russian center Arvidas Sabonis, then considered one of the best amateur big men in the world.

Herrmann was now the head coach and had seen how David had developed as a player and a person.

"I think the better David became, the more he felt he wanted to keep improving," Coach Herrmann said. "When I asked him his goals in the preseason, he told me right away that he wanted to be college Player of the Year."

The Navy team had lost its number-two and -three scorers, so there would be an even bigger burden on David as a senior. He showed he was ready in the opener against a good North Carolina State team. The Middies lost 86-84, but David scored 36 points. Two games later he hit for 43 in a 91-90 overtime victory over Michigan State. On offense he looked almost unstoppable.

Big games kept coming. Against James Madison, David scored 45 points and grabbed 21 rebounds. He had 44 points in an upset loss to Drexel in which the rest of his teammates totaled just 36 points among them. Some nights it seemed as if David were a one-man gang. But he always worked very well with point guard Doug Wojcik.

"We had a keen sense of awareness between us," Wojcik said. "All David had to do was lift his head a little or his eyes toward the bucket, and I'd throw him an alley-oop. Then he'd go get it and finish the play."

David's outstanding talent on the basketball court was attracting a great deal of attention. More and more people asked him for autographs. Writers and reporters wanted interviews with him. He was often asked about his future in pro ball. Through it all he remained polite and courteous, often trying to juggle a very busy schedule. He also continued to earn top grades in all his courses.

"David could have been very demanding to coach because of his status and stature," said Pete Herrmann. "But he was simply the same David Robinson I had met as a senior in high school. He had grown as a person greatly, but never demanded anything and always gave of himself."

Opposing teams keyed on David his senior year. He was often double- and triple-teamed by defenses that tried to stop him. Opposing players often tried to push, bump, and elbow him. Even Coach Herrmann said that David took a lot of physical abuse on the court.

"But he always played with the same demeanor," the coach said. "He didn't show much emotion on the court."

In January of David's senior year there were some changes in Navy rules that would affect David's future. Now when David graduated he would be commissioned in the Naval Reserve instead of the regular Navy. That meant David would only have to serve two years active duty

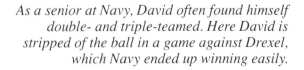

As a senior at Navy, David often found himself double- and triple-teamed. Here David is stripped of the ball in a game against Drexel, which Navy ended up winning easily.

instead of five. The reason was that he had become too tall to serve as an unrestricted line officer.

It also meant there was more of a chance that David could play pro ball. "Two years is better than five years," he said. "I'm glad the decision has been made, and I know what my future is going to be."

David was the type of person who would have accepted whatever the Navy ruled. But by this time it was no secret that he wanted to play pro ball. It was also no secret that the NBA wanted him. He had become so good that he was looked at as a future pro superstar.

But first he had a season to finish. David put on another incredible performance in a losing effort against powerful Kentucky. He had 45 points, 14 rebounds, and had blocked 10 shots. Even teams good enough to beat Navy couldn't stop David Robinson.

Navy finished the regular 1987 season with a 26-5 record, winning their conference championship once more. But in the first round of the NCAA tourney Navy lost to the University of Michigan 97-82. Once again the Middies couldn't deal with a fast-paced running game. But David was all over the court, scoring on a variety of jump shots, drives, hooks, and dunks. He used every move he had learned in four years to go over and through the Michigan team. It just wasn't quite enough.

David had made his final game as a collegian perhaps his very best. He hit 22 of 37 field goal tries as he finished with a career-best 50 points. For the season he averaged 28.2 points a game, third best among Division I players.

Coach Pete Herrmann has a kind word for David after Navy was beaten by Michigan, 97-82, eliminating the Middies from the 1987 NCAA tournament.

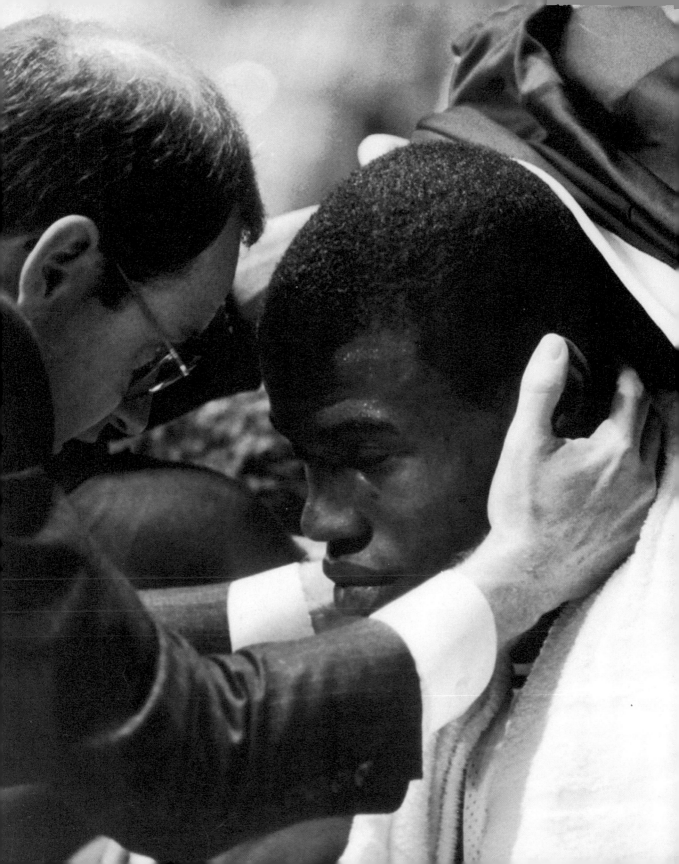

He also grabbed 11.8 rebounds a game. That was fourth best in the country. And his 144 blocked shots was once more the nation's best.

He also set numerous Naval Academy records. His 2,669 career points were tenth best in NCAA history. His national record of 207 blocked shots in a season still stands. During his Navy career David had 30 games in which he scored 30 points or more, including 15 in his senior year alone.

David was a consensus all-American, named as the center on every major poll. And that wasn't all. He also realized his final goal: David was named college basketball's Player of the Year.

WAITING FOR A ROOKIE

In June 1987 David Robinson graduated from the Naval Academy. He was awarded a bachelor's degree in mathematics and would be going to the Navy submarine base at Kings Bay, Georgia. There, David would be an assistant resident officer in charge of construction. His pay from the Navy would be $315.23 a week.

But before he even started there was a good chance that a lot more money could come his way. It was almost time for the National Basketball Association draft. There were seven teams in the lottery for the number-one pick. They were the teams with the poorest records from the year

In April 1987, David was given the John R. Wooden Award as college basketball's top student/athlete. Presenting the award is the former legendary UCLA coach, John Wooden, after whom the award is named.

before. They would choose players in an order determined by a random drawing—a lottery.

Both the team with the top choice and David would have to decide what to do. David knew he could not play in the NBA for two years because of the Navy rule. Even if he were picked, he didn't have to sign. He could wait for the draft again in two years. Any team wanting to pick him also knew he could not play for them for two years.

The team that got the right for the first pick in 1987 turned out to be the San Antonio Spurs. The Spurs didn't waste a second. As soon as they knew they had the number-one pick, they chose David Robinson. The team felt that even if they had to wait two years, David would be worth it.

Everyone knew the Spurs needed a center badly. The ball club had a record of 28-54 in 1986-1987, its worst ever. The fans were staying away, and there was talk of moving the team to another city. So David was looked upon as a possible savior for the franchise.

At first David said he hadn't decided whether to sign or not. He needed more time. He went to work with the Navy and kept the Spurs on hold. Then, in November 1987, a big announcement came out of San Antonio. David had signed a huge contract to begin play with the Spurs in the 1989-1990 season. It was a $26 million pact spread over eight years. Although David would not join the team for nearly two years, he was already one of the highest paid players in the NBA.

The David Robinson wait began. And the more the Spurs struggled, the more San Antonio fans looked forward to David. In 1987-1988 the team was 31-51, and a year later it finished at 21-61, the worst record in franchise history. But the Spurs had a new coach that year, the always successful Larry Brown. Now they wanted their center.

In the two years between graduating from Navy and joining the Spurs in the fall of 1989, David did not play much basketball. He had played for the United States Olympic team in 1988 but didn't look very sharp. The U.S. team finished a disappointing third that summer at Seoul, South Korea. David averaged just 12.8 points and 6 rebounds a game.

On May 19, 1989 David was discharged from the Navy. He started getting ready for the NBA almost immediately. His first step was to join the Spurs rookie camp that summer. It didn't take long for his game to start coming back.

"I really don't think I have to change any of my basic skills," he said at the

In 1988 Robinson played with the United States Olympic team. Here he operates in an early-round game against Spain in which he scored 16 points.

time. "I have to build up my intensity and then use my skills, something I've always done. I also plan to run all the time and beat my opponent up and down the floor. When I run like I can, nobody can run with me."

At the same time that David was getting ready for his first pro camp, the Spurs were building a better team to work with him. They traded for 6-foot-9 (206-centimeter) forward Terry Cummings, a top scorer and experienced veteran. Then they drafted 6-foot-8 (203-centimeter) forward Sean Elliott of Arizona. Like Robinson, Elliott had been College Player of the Year and was expected to become a top pro. Veteran point guard Maurice Cheeks was brought in to team with young Willie Anderson in the backcourt. The final piece to the puzzle was the big center. And he was coming in, as usual, with a goal.

"I want to be one of the top four centers in the league," Robinson said. "My only other goal is to improve each game all year. I'm ready now. Two years away have sometimes seemed like ten. But the closer I get, the more anticipation I feel."

ROOKIE OF THE YEAR

David Robinson came to training camp in great shape and ready to go. He had worked with weights during his two-year Navy hitch and was stronger than ever. He was still slim, with a 33-inch (84 centimeter) waist. But his

David drives around Houston's Akeem Olajuwon
during a Spurs victory over the Rockets.

arms were muscular. NBA action can be rough, and Robinson wasn't about to be pushed around. He was ready to do battle with other top centers, like Patrick Ewing of the Knicks and Akeem Olajuwon of the Houston Rockets.

He played very well in the pre-season, and finally it was time for his first game. It came on November 4, 1989, as 15,868 fans jammed into the HemisFair Arena in San Antonio to watch Robinson and the Spurs meet Earvin "Magic" Johnson and the Los Angeles Lakers. The Lakers were then one of the best teams in the league.

It didn't take the rookie center long to show the Lakers and everyone else that he was going to be a force. In the first period the Lakers tried to muscle him. They were testing his toughness right away. Robinson simply took the fouls and made his foul shots. The Lakers saw he couldn't be intimidated.

The game stayed close right into the third period. The Spurs had a 72-70 lead, but Los Angeles had the basketball. Magic Johnson, already one of the greatest players of all time, drove down the middle to the hoop. When Magic released a short floater, there was David Robinson, leaping high in the air and swatting the ball away. It was his first NBA block and it triggered a 6-0 Spurs's run. That gave San Antonio a lead it would not lose.

The Spurs went on to win, 106-98, with Robinson scoring a team-best 23 points and leading both clubs with 17 rebounds. It was as good a debut as anyone could have hoped for. Robinson had been the dominant player on the floor. Even Magic Johnson was impressed.

"Some rookies are never really rookies," Magic said, after the game. "Robinson is one of them."

He certainly was not an ordinary rookie. First of all, he was very talented. He was already getting the kind of attention from the media that was usually reserved for superstars.

"All the attention I've received is a little bit embarrassing," Robinson said. "All I'm trying to do is make my place in the league."

He also continued to show his intellectual side. He didn't eat, sleep, and live only basketball. Robinson was still a young man of many interests.

"I feel like I'm growing again, changing, and expanding as a person," he said. "I'm reading a lot, teaching myself to play the piano, even writing some songs."

Robinson was soon writing his own story around the NBA. He began putting up numbers similar to the top centers in the league. And more importantly, the Spurs were winning. By the end of January 1990 the team was 29-13, with the league-best 19-1 record at home. No team could take the Spurs for granted now.

Around the league, people were already putting Robinson in the same category as Ewing and Olajuwon. Forward Charles Barkley of Philadelphia, an all-star in his own right, said this about David: "He's going to be a monster. He can do it all—play defense, shoot, rebound, and block shots. Plus, he's the fastest big man I've ever played against."

In February, David played in the NBA All-Star Game, scoring 15 points and grabbing 10 rebounds in just 25 minutes of action.

"I've played with the best there is and did okay," David said. "I was a little nervous before the game, but when I got in I felt good and gained confidence."

Robinson played even better the second half of the year. He helped the Spurs finish the year with a club record 56-26 mark and a divisional title. They had the fourth-best record in the entire league. That wasn't all. By finishing a full 35 games better than they had the year before, the Spurs had made the biggest turnaround in NBA history from one season to the next. David Robinson, of course, had played a major role in the turnaround.

Robinson finished his first pro season in 1989-1990 scoring 1,993 points in 82 games for a 24.3 average. That was tenth best in the league. He finished second to Olajuwon in rebounding with 983 boards for a 12.0 average. He was third in blocked shots with an average of 3.89, finishing behind Olajuwon and Ewing. There was little doubt that he belonged right up there with the other two.

As the Spurs got ready for the playoffs, there was an announcement from NBA headquarters. David Robinson had been named NBA Rookie of the Year.

ON TO GREATNESS

With Robinson having a great first year, the Spurs felt they had a good chance in the 1990 playoffs. When they beat the Denver Nuggets three straight in the first round, they felt even better. Then they had to meet the tough Portland Trail Blazers. The Blazers were 59-23 in the regular season. They were led by superstar Clyde Drexler and other fine players like Terry Porter and Jerome Kersey.

It was a very tough series. Almost all the Spurs played well. Robinson, Cummings, Anderson, and guard Rod Strickland, who had come over in a trade for Cheeks—all had big games. But Portland was just as good. Finally it came down to a seventh and deciding contest. The winner would advance to the conference finals.

The game was played at Portland and was close all the way. Neither team could take a big lead. It was tense, tight playoff basketball with excellent defense and a lot of banging underneath. The game was tied at the end of regulation time and went into overtime. Still both teams battled. The game was still knotted with 30 seconds left in overtime. Rod Strickland of the Spurs had the ball. One more hoop might win it.

But Strickland got too fancy. He tried an over-the-head pass without looking, and Portland intercepted. The Blazers came back up court and quickly scored. Seconds later it was over. Portland had a 108-105 victory to eliminate the Spurs.

In ten playoff games, David Robinson averaged 24.3 points, 12 rebounds, and 4 blocks. These statistics were very close to his regular-season stats. That showed how consistent Robinson was as a rookie.

He had earned respect from everyone. Phoenix Suns' coach Cotton Fitzsimmons showed the respect he had for Robinson's talents when he said, "The only team that has a chance [to dominate] in the 1990s is San Antonio because of David Robinson. He's the greatest impact player the league has seen since Kareem Abdul-Jabbar."

At the beginning of the 1990-1991 season, the man they now called Mister Robinson or the Admiral was at it again. He was beginning to put

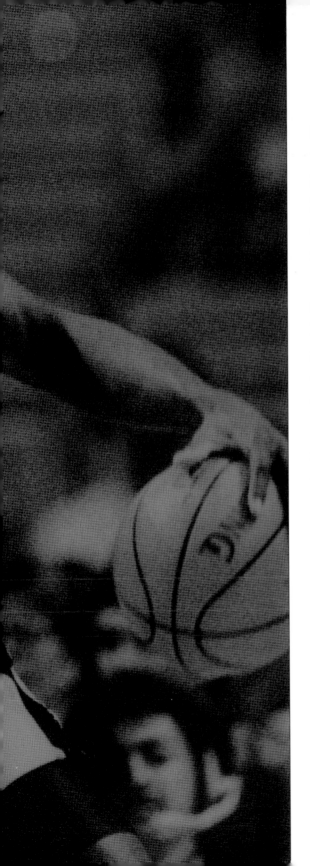

together some big games. His 40-point, 14-rebound, 5-block night against Phoenix drew rave reviews around the league. He was also leading the Spurs to another great start. The team was 21-7 in the early going and a threat to win it all.

After Robinson had a 35-point, 16-rebound game against Atlanta, the Hawks' superstar Dominique Wilkins said, "They talk about Ewing and Olajuwon, but I see David doing things they can't do."

Robinson continued to play outstanding basketball. Like all great centers, there was no doubt that he could dominate a game. In fact, it was beginning to look as if David Robinson was already the best center in the NBA. So it was not surprising when he was named as starter for the Western Conference team in the mid-season All-Star game.

David was the fastest center in the league and could handle the ball very well for a player his size. Here he performs almost as a guard in a game against the Denver Nuggets.

Toward the end of February, the Admiral was leading the league in rebounding and in blocked shots. His scoring average was at 26.1 points per game and the Spurs were battling the Utah Jazz for the Midwest Division lead. San Antonio kept playing well even though several players were hurt during parts of the season. Robinson stayed healthy and the team won four of their last five games to top the division with a 55-27 mark.

"I'm very proud of this team," Coach Brown said. "With all the injuries and everything else that's happened, we've done well, if not better than we could have expected."

David Robinson was one of the few Spurs who played in all 82 games. He averaged 25.6 points a game, ninth best in the league. He also led the league with a 13.0 rebounding average and wound up second in blocks with a 3.9 mark. He was named the center on the 1991 All-NBA team as well as on the All-Defensive team. Not many players make both those teams in the same year.

But there was disappointment, too. In the first round of the playoffs, the Spurs were upset by the Golden State Warriors. Golden State took the best-of-five series, 3-1. San Antonio was eliminated and Robinson took it quite hard.

Robinson was never one to make excuses. "We just let them get aggressive and take the game away from us," he said. "I don't feel I fulfilled my responsibility. I have to take a lot of responsibility for this team. I like to

By the 1991 playoffs David was considered one of the NBA's best. Here he scores in a game against Phoenix, going over Mark West (left) and Kurt Rambis as if they weren't there.

In the 1991 playoffs he mixes it up with several Golden State Warriors as they battle for a rebound.

think I have an impact on the team, so you like to play well in these games. It's very disappointing."

He might have felt he had let this team down, but other NBA stars knew he hadn't. Even though he was one of the best at his position, he couldn't do it alone.

"You can't win with one guy anymore," said star Philadelphia forward Charles Barkley. "You need a supporting cast. Coaching is too good these days to let one big superstar beat you."

That was true. The Spurs had a good team, but the feeling was that they needed a couple more solid players to challenge the top few teams in the league. They came back with pretty much the same group in 1991-1992 and began to play good, but not great, ball once again. But any team with David Robinson in the lineup had a chance to win the championship.

Robinson was in the midst of another great season. In the eyes of many he was now the best all-around center in the league. He was the quickest and the best shot-blocker. Some might still choose Ewing or Olajuwon, but more and more were beginning to like the Admiral's game.

It wasn't an easy season for the Spurs. Coach Brown was fired in mid-season and replaced by Bob Bass, a former Spurs coach. Then, in late March, with the team trying to regroup, Robinson was hurt for the first time in his career. He tore ligaments in his left thumb. It was a serious injury and he had to have surgery right away. Although he didn't make it back in time for the playoffs, Robinson still led the league in blocked shots and was named NBA Defensive Player of the Year.

The Spurs knew that David Robinson would return. And all of basketball knew that he still could be the center of the 1990s. Robinson has come a long way in a short time. When he was in high school, basketball was just a hobby. A few years later, he was the best college player in the land. Ever since then he has worked hard to become better and better.

But Robinson has always remained an all-around person who still has many interests. He has been part of the "I Have a Dream Foundation" that provides scholarships for certain elementary school kids who graduate from high school and qualify to attend a university. He has been a caring man who, when he sponsored a fifth-grade class at the Gates Elementary School in San Antonio, told them, "I hope you don't mind, but I'm going to think of you guys as my kids."

David Robinson has continued to live up to the standards he has always set for himself. He has been a great basketball player. More importantly, he has been a kind and intelligent person. This has made his father very proud.

"I'm just so pleased that David has had such an impact on people's lives, especially the kids," Ambrose Robinson has said. "I'm also so happy that he's remained the same person. He's handled his success—the money and the attention—very well. What you see is what you get."

And, what people have seen on the basketball court has been one of the best centers in the game.

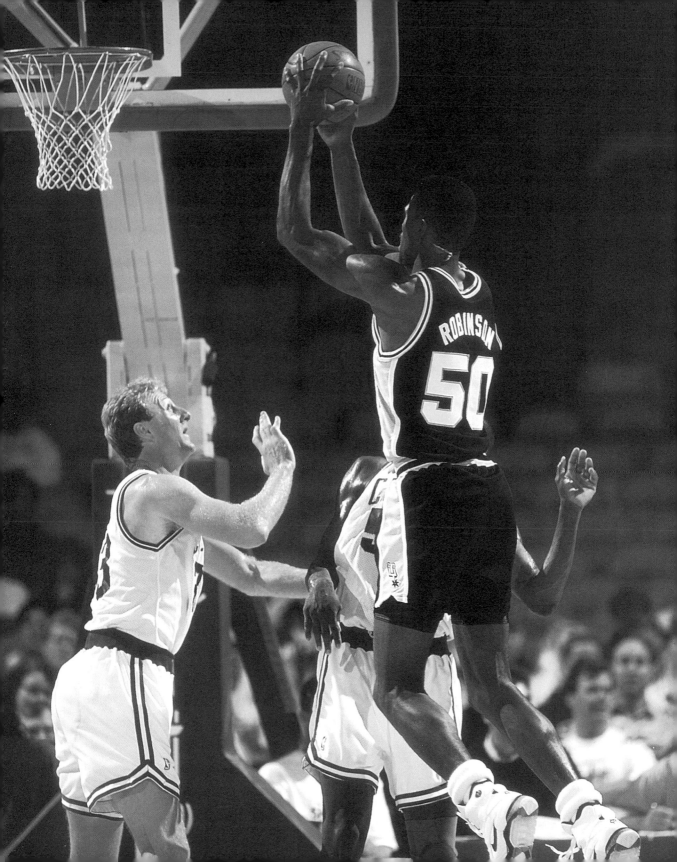

DAVID ROBINSON: HIGHLIGHTS

1965	Born on August 16 in Virginia Beach, Virginia.
1982	Moves to Manassas, Virginia, and begins playing basketball at Osbourn Park High School.
1983	Enters the United States Naval Academy.
1985	Becomes Navy starting center as a sophomore and leads the Middies to the NCAA tournament for the first time in 25 years. Named the Eastern Collegiate Athletic Conference South Player of the Year.
1986	Named first team All-American. Sets national record of 207 blocked shots in a season. Leads the U.S. national team to victory in the World Championships in Spain.
1987	Achieved career-high 50 points in NCAA tournament game. Named as center on the All-American team. Named college basketball Player of the Year. Graduates the Naval Academy in June, and is stationed at Kings Bay, Georgia. Becomes the NBA number-one draft pick when chosen by the San Antonio Spurs. Signs with the Spurs.
1988	Plays with the U.S. Olympic team.
1989	Discharged from the Navy on May 19. First pro game with the San Antonio Spurs on November 4.
1990	Plays in the NBA All-Star Game. Leads the Spurs to win the division title. Named NBA Rookie of the Year.
1991	Named starting center for Western Conference in the NBA All-Star game. Named center on the All-NBA team and the All-Defensive Team.
1992	Injures left thumb, has surgery, and misses the final part of the season. Named NBA Defensive Player of the Year. Plays with U.S. Olympic "Dream Team" in Barcelona; wins Gold Medal.

FIND OUT MORE

Aaseng, Nathan. *Basketball's Playmakers*. Minneapolis, Minn.: Lerner, 1983.

Anderson, Dave. *The Story of Basketball*. New York: Morrow Junior Books, 1988.

Bloom, Marc. *Basketball*. New York: Scholastic, Inc., 1991.

Duden, Jane and Susan Osberg. *Basketball*. New York: Macmillan, 1991.

Miller, Dawn M. *David Robinson: Backboard Admiral*. Minneapolis, Minn.: Lerner, 1992.

Savage, Jim. *The Force: Basketball's David Robinson*. New York: Dell, 1992.

How to write to
David Robinson:

David Robinson
8632 Fredericksberg Rd.
Suite 209
San Antonio, Texas 78240

INDEX